Give the Bard a Tetanus Shot

poems

V.C. Myers

Give the Bard a Tetanus Shot ©**2024, 2019** by **V.C. Myers.**
Published in the United States by Vegetarian Alcoholic Press, Inc.
Not one part of this work may be reproduced without expressed
written consent from the author. For more information, please write
V.A. Press, 643 South 2nd Street, Milwaukee, WI 53204

ISBN: 978-1-7338483-6-7

for Mom, Lori, Cayla, and Marisa

&

for Brendan, for everything

Contents

I

No Trespassing	15
Give the Bard a Tetanus Shot	16
Formative	17
Fire-tongued Labyrinth	18
Snow Cream	19
Trestle	20
Watershed	21

II

The Stone Age	25
Tilt-A-Whirl	26
For Want of an Ark	28
The Old Toot-N-Tellem	30
Flood Diorama	32
Baptism by Fire	33
Cover Us With Mountains	34
Give the Bard a Break	36
The Farm	37
His Orchestra	38
Hibernation	39

III

Hinterland	43
Potluck	44
Grandma's Texas Sheet Cake	46
The Great Depression	47
Out of the Frying Pan into the Fire	48
Stuck in Blue Spring State Park, Florida	50
Whitetails in Wildflowers	52
Catharsis	53
Non-conformist Northern Flicker	54
Broken Wing Act	55

IV

The Snow Angel	59
American Gothic	60
Lessons in Mining	62
The Ghosts We Inherit	64
Ship of Theseus	65
#NoFilter	66

V

Neighborhood Watch	71
Shadowbox	72
Bonfires	73
The Evening News	74
Ism	75
Democratic Pomp	76
The Ethics of Horses	77
Avaricious Symbiosis	78
Give the Bard a Hep A Shot	79

VI

In Search of a Karass	83
Driftwood	84
Solastalgia	85
Crossroads	86
Glendalough	87
Seafarers	88
The Parting Glass	89

Playlist
Acknowledgements
Poet's Bio
Notes

Give the Bard
a Tetanus Shot

———————————

I am Appalachia…
How can you find rapport with me—
You, who never stood in the bowels of hell,
Never felt a mountain shake and open its jaws
To partake of human sacrifice?

-Muriel Miller Dressler

I

No Trespassing

A small, solitary carousel horse stands
impaled on a rusted pole
tangled in barbed wire and tall grass,
decayed by flood water and mud,
its black paint peeled away, revealing
a white plastic skull, one-eyed and
screaming.

Give the Bard a Tetanus Shot

How the hell am I supposed to write poetry
in the dirty, crowded parking lot
                     of the local Piggly Wiggly—
hunkered down and avoiding eye contact
with checkout clerks on their smoke breaks
and drug dealers, faking car trouble, waiting
for their drop?   Not to mention the zombies,
high on meth, ghost-eyed, and shuffle-limping along
the muddy, littered riverbank over there, where
the kudzu's too dry and dead to bother creeping,
and late November has stripped the trees bare,
revealing a monstrous eyesore in the distance—
a rusted out corrugated metal tank, a wraith
of the old, abandoned water tower, which once
nourished our forgotten fossil of a town.
Classic European poets found their inspiration
among the crumbling ruins of ancient castle stone.
New York City poets see their muse's reflection
in the shiny glass of towering skyscrapers.
While here I sit in Appalachia—the point where
the Bible Belt's buckle ever tightens the Rust Belt—
surrounded by nothing but decay and desperation.

Formative

The teacher lured
the class with
lollipops, marching
them, single-file,
to the cemetery.
Haunting takes
so many forms,
lingering like the
bitter aftertaste
of sour hard candy
swallowed in a field
of unmarked graves.

Fire-tongued Labyrinth

I was born in a blue field
after the circus
        came to town.

     Doves flew
from my sister's throat as
she swallowed   bright
        stars.

                The stag
rested   in the hunter's horn,
sounding out   sour notes of
        kudzu.

Fireflies have no faith
          nor need of
sun and fluorescent
     bulbs.

     Whisper
indoors, the walls
          have ears and flies
stuck   in their ointment.

Lions are leaving
            my skin
in scars, in droves   of
     horse-drawn carriages.

Snow Cream

for Mom

Winter hit us hard in '84. No power, no running
water, a gas stove our only source of heat.

My father bundled me up in my sister's snow-
suit and pink scarf to take me "sledding"

on a black trash bag while my mother wrapped
herself in her own tattered coat and boots. A pail

of plastic in her gloved hands, she gathered snow
from the back yard. She melted and boiled her spoils

atop the stove for more practical purposes, but saved
the rest to mix with vanilla and sugar. When she lay

the bowl of homemade "snow cream" before me,
I thought she was magic. And she was. She was.

Trestle

This is the way we were: in our growing up and in our marrying and in our living and in our dying.

-Thornton Wilder. *Our Town.*

Wild tangles of glistening
blackberry bushes border
a path of unwieldy weeds,
rusted rails, and rotted ties—
ruins of a train track running
across the old trestle bridge
into the dark, open mouth of a
looming tunnel whose whistles
of warning have long been
silenced. No sound remains
save the faint fluttering of
wings—a cave cocoon of bats
in slumber awaits the dusk
descent of the sun to lure them
skyward, susurrus silhouettes
swiftly rising in the alpenglow
as our quixotic clan meanders
barefoot along the sandy creek-
bed, skipped stones rippling
reflections of our fresh faces
smiling in summer light. Before
life reduced us, subtracting
our numbers, one   by one.
Before we knew grief.
Before the word "family"
carved canyons of pain in
the spaces between our hands.

Watershed

*After the 1,000-Year Flood
of Elk River, WV, June, 2016*

Never give your heart to a body
of water. Like a wayward lover,
it will only hurt you in the end.

I was courted in adolescence, bare
skin in a cool, calm cove. I poured
tears of grief in supplication and

found solace in a glacial white lull,
pain floated away in paper lanterns.
Sounds of weariness, of wonder.

One morning, I awoke to find
the river curling around my bed.
The bank broken in wild abandon.

Terror too terrible a kiss. A bond
asunder in fear, in uncertainty.
The mirthless waltz of water.

II

The Stone Age

After the Mid-Atlantic Derecho, June 2012

The trees were the first to feel it,
boughs bent, swirling furious fists
of lush foliage, twirling green leaves
up to reveal silvery underbellies,
the surest sign of brewing rain.
Wind shivered the river and whipped
the pines, whirling them in tight circles,
wringing them like mops in buckets
of rain as thunder roared from within
the earth itself. Lightning sliced
a weeping willow in half, dropping
its sad arms to split the wooden fence
in the front yard, sending splinters
and sparks through spreading shadows.
A freight train of black clouds barreled
across the valley, chewing powerlines,
and cell towers, leaving us cowering
beneath bridges and clinging to floors
in dark houses. Calendar pages torn
without light or air conditioning in
an unrelenting wave of inhuman heat
and human rage over dwindling supplies.
Then, from dusty mountain hollows,
emerged the wise women, leading
their kin down to the river to teach
us the old ways, their wrinkled hands
working out the history written within
their bones, reminding us that we were
once Earth's children: fed with fresh-
caught fish, drinking pure, rushing
water, scrubbing soiled rags clean with
washboards and rough river stones.

Tilt-A-Whirl

After the Eastern Tornado Outbreak, June 1998

Trapped, in our Sunday best,
    in standstill traffic; as
    rain raised the river to tickle
    the road beneath our tires;
at the mercy of that horrid alarm, its
    intermittent, teeth-grinding cacophony
        rattling the car radio,
    the monotonous voice,
so nonchalant in its declaration that, no,
contrary to countless tests of this, the
Emergency Broadcast System, blaring
    in our jaded ears for the entirety of
    our varying ages—my baby boomer mother,
        my sister and I covering
        Generation X and Y,
        my Millennial baby niece
        crying in her car seat—
    This. Is. Not. A. Test.
        And there was no escape
from the tornado barreling down
that very highway in our direction.
The only question:
        would the twister reach us before the river?
That slow motion race between forces
of nature held us captive, frozen in terror. I reached
for the passenger door just as the car leapt forward,
as traffic gave way to hope, and we spied two figures
in bright yellow raincoats braving the storm to shout:
        Take the next exit, no matter what!

    Later, we huddled
beneath a darkened underpass, that portentous exit,
watching tornadoes   dance their twisting destruction
at all four corners of horizon.   Stuck
in the storm's eye, the heart   of its ravenous compass,
we thanked God
       for those highway prophets and, even more,
       for our having heeded their clarion call.

For Want of an Ark

*After the 1,000-Year Flood
of Elk River, WV, June, 2016*

The river swelled silently in the night,
    swiftly swallowing our small town
in a filthy sea of flood-water and mud,
    leaving only our trembling bodies
and sobbing prayers for so many
    neighbors swept away as we slept.

Rescue rafts float up flooded highways.
    Helicopters drop supplies from the sky
to survivors stranded on their rooftops.
    Houses uprooted, crushed against bridges,
debris dragged downstream to trim trees
    along the riverbank with ornamental rot.

Muscular brown water thrusts open
    school doors, walking halls, slipping into
lockers to steal secret notes and textbooks,
    smashing trophy cases, battering black-
boards with teachers' desks, jumping
    up to clear scoreboards. Nothin' but net.

Churches and cemeteries desecrated,
    the unrepentant river preying on pews,
baptizing Bibles and hymnals, toppling
    steeples, unearthing and emptying graves
to fill their vacancies with flood victims.
    Nothing sacred.   No one spared.

Do any human beings ever realize life
    while they live it—every, every minute?[1]
Before the great clockwork of memory,
    so finely tuned, wound, and passed down
through a century of generations, grinds
    to a cataclysmic halt, rusting in sorrow.

The Old Toot-N-Tellem

*After the 1,000-Year Flood
of Elk River, WV, June, 2016*

After the flood, the old folks talk
      about climate change, about loss.
*I never believed in global warmin',
      but the river ain't never got so high!*

Neighbors who survived gather to watch
      FEMA workers mark condemned houses
with large, red, spray-painted numbers—
      bullseyes for their bulldozers to plow down.

#K57 was the old Toot-N-Tellem, the heart
      of the community for half a century—
still referred to as the central landmark
      whenever locals gave out directions.

The old folks say it was *the place to be*
      in the '50s. The quintessential drive-in—
girls in ponytails and poodle skirts serving
      trays of burgers and shakes on rollerskates.

One skating waitress was the owner's daughter,
      who met the love of her life through the
window of his car. They became high school
      sweethearts, marrying after graduation.

Now an elderly couple with grown kids
        and grandkids, they stand, holding hands,
teary-eyed and sentimental, reminiscing
        about the good old days—saying goodbye

to the small, square relic of their romance as
        it is demolished, along with a lifetime
of joyous communal memories. The
        empty lot left lying open like a grave.

Flood Diorama

Swamp   bones
     and chicken
            feet
bloated
     flesh
     in muddy creek

Hush now,
      she's a comin'
creepin' up
      from behind

Baptism by Fire

*After the Elk River, WV Chemical Spill /
Water Crisis, January, 2014*

Cleanliness is truly next to Godliness
here, in West *By God* Virginia—
where coal and chemicals are
worshipped as deities.

Our water source was contaminated
with 4-Methylcyclohexanemethanol—
a licorice-scented chemical
used to clean that divine coal.

We are now immaculate!
Holy coals burning so bright—
in our scorched skin,
in our blackened lungs.

We are so blessed!
to breathe at all here in Chemical Valley—
a sunken kingdom crowned
by coal mines and chemical plants.

I once believed
the Golden Ratio was God's fingerprint—
before the chemicals branded my skin
with his cleansing touch.

It's hard to see sacred geometry now,
to feel beyond the pain of betrayal—
that holy fire we drank up
in full, unguarded faith.

Cover Us With Mountains

*After the Elk River, WV Chemical Spill /
Water Crisis, January, 2014*

Chemical Valley's cup runneth over
with sweet poison secretly stored
along the snowy river bank, in
ancient tanks, rusted and ruptured,
spilling licorice-scented, toxic terror
into the unsuspecting, unprotected
source of our local water supply.

The air soon smells like a candy shop
as our hands blister beneath the tap.
Trusting tongues and vulnerable flesh
shall reap unknown consequences.
Till then, we pray for mercy and beg
for clean water at neighborly wells.

The lonely walk of troubled kin into
dark river waters left his parents torn
like paper dolls; their tears pooling
on their kitchen table beneath
his mocking photograph smile.

When my father's ticking heart
betrayed him in the Texas heat,
his widow's telephone dirge
set a wildfire across state lines.
We are bereft ash smoldering
in his ghost-rippled wake.

More friendly fires followed:
self-inflicted gunshot escape
from swarming uniform blue
after domestic violence catalyst,
blood mingling with snow,
between houses, crimson cold.

Now our boy gasps for life, marrow
deep, in cruel hospital cage.
There's been far too much death
harvested by this unrelenting Winter,
this ravenous reaping machine.

When sorrows come, they come
not single spies, but in battalions[2]
and we are under heavy fire
without bullet or shield. We claw
for higher ground and weep
for all that we have lost.

Give the Bard a Break

You can have it all.
My empire of dirt.

-Nine Inch Nails

I've crafted a world
for myself, a private pearl
in this festering oyster.

Forcing my way through
each day of work, this
maddening mediocrity.

Rushing home to be
quiet, to be still, to be
a poet, to be myself.

I love my mountains,
my people—their strength
and fierce endurance.

But I'm tired of bearing
witness to their sorrows
with the written word.

The Farm

In memory of my father

My soul cries an empty field, flooded
by the broken dam of my father's death.

A torrent of memory muddies tender soil
where once stood the family farmhouse.

The echo of a nightjar fills the evening air,
carrying me back to an enchanted night

held in his arms under a sky full of stars
and the Whippoorwill's song of sorrow.

His Orchestra

In memory of Greg Keenan

Cruelty is not the only sound
whose echo rises
from the canyon.

Kindness conducts a call
and response, one note
answered by a symphony.

When a good man dies, his deeds
are sung out by a choir
of grateful mourners.

A thousand voices singing
in unison. A thousand eyes
weeping a single tear.

A thousand hearts beating
as one. The drum he made
with generous hands.

Hibernation

Winter is the hardest season;
harsh winds shaking naked trees
before a blanket of snow falls
to cover the cold, dead ground.

The gray overshadows memories of
childhood play wrapped in warmth.
Clouds obscure the mountain view
as shadows seep into the barren fields.

Yet soon will fall the gentle shroud;
to smooth the lines of rugged earth
with silence, pale and calming;
to hush the soil beneath its weight.

And then, amidst the powder white,
a bud will bloom without fanfare
to herald the dawn of Spring,
awakening us from hibernation.

III

Hinterland

We love the things we love for what they are

                                          -Robert Frost

Dirt roads sprawl   penciled lines
on maps   of countless corn fields,
pinned up by wooden pegs: barns
branded black   by *Mail Pouch* tobacco.

We call our vacation homes   *camps*
and plant 'em knee deep in mud   along
the riverbank   obscured by overgrown
weeds   and stagnant mosquito ponds.

Picnic paper plates   piled high,
we dangle bare feet   over
old, abandoned   riverboat docks,
skimmin'   green summer water.

The sweet smell   of honeysuckle
perfumes   the hot, sticky air
better   than a store bought bottle
and the buzzin' bumble bees   testify.

Sharp wind whispers   winter's sneakin'
up behind   our sunburnt backs like
snakes in high grass   slithering
back home   to the river.

Potluck

for Margy

What the hell was it?

That flesh-colored lump
on the end of the table.

                Surrounded
by baked ham and baked goods,
potato salad, and fresh rolls.

Its gelatinous bulk   marring
an otherwise fine spread.

The ugliest shape,   the ugliest shade
of Pepto-Bismol pink,   ringed
in a toxic yellow neon topping.

The smiling server's spoon
plopped a dollop   of mystery
on my tray.
              I carried it away
with no intention to consume it, but

  potluck luck   is always bad,

so I soon found myself sitting
next to the bouffanted chef of this
           culinary monstrosity.

You got my famous spam loaf!

Her cooing delight   triggered
my people-pleasing nature.

Scooping and swallowing a small,
spammy bite   in one swift,
wincing motion,   I gagged

as the slimy ball slid   from my
betrayed tongue   down my
disbelieving, contracting throat,
landing   with a palpable thud
in my churning, burning belly.

Plastering a plastic smile
upon my puckered lips,   lying
through my sticky, sour teeth,
I remarked on the unique tang
of Chef Beehive's spam loaf.

The pride of her smile   as big
as her teased up tower of hair,
her gravelly voice dropped
to an excited whisper:

That's my secret ingredient:
            lemon jelly!

Grandma's Texas Sheet Cake

In memory of Naomi Ernestine Maloney

I wish she was here
to tell me   what I did wrong.
I followed her recipe

word for word—scrawled
in pencil   on an old index card,
passed down   two generations.

Her curling handwriting   faded
and chocolate-stained,   warped
by decades   of loving use.

Grandma's Texas Sheet Cake was
perfectly flat,   perfectly baked,
perfectly iced.   Perfect.

My cake   is an ugly, crooked lump.
Missing the magic   ingredient
only she could give it.   Just like me.

The Great Depression

An antique photograph shows
  my grandmother   walking
in a post-Armistice city,

her hurried heels tapping
crowded cobblestones,   her
harried hands   clasping

paper bags of fresh produce.
Some stranger captured her
in sepia,   immortalizing her

hourglass figure,   her flaxen
hair, her alabaster skin,   her
pouty lips and ageless beauty

perpetually frozen   in a frown
born   of secret, domestic strains.
Her husband,   distant enough

at home,   flown further afield
on a foreign front,   leaving her
behind   with an unwieldy brood:

    six sets of his Irish eyes,
    six small, hungry bellies,
    six mouths begging for

food, warmth, and a kind of
maternal love and comfort
she could no longer provide.

Out of the Frying Pan into the Fire

After the Seminole Woods,
Florida Wildfires, June, 1998

We smelled the smoke
before we heard the knock.

It was just like TV, where
a tall, muscular firefighter
commands: *You have to*
evacuate, the fire is closing in.

Behind his handsome head,
at the edge of the woods
surrounding my grandparents'
retirement home,   we saw

a colossal charcoal column
of smoke   billowing skyward
like a mushroom cloud.
Grandpa could barely stand

from his advanced leukemia,
so Mom and Grandma stood
on each side of him   to support
his walker shuffle out to the car.

I stuffed a suitcase full   with
as many of their possessions as
I could, then ran   out to ride
shotgun as my mother drove.

From the backseat,   Grandma
turned to look behind,   tears
in her eyes   at yet another home
she was forced to leave behind.

A lifetime of hardship had not
prepared her   for this final loss.
Fear of fire was more potent   than
all the famine, drought, floods, and

grief   she had already survived.
As the car braked for a red light,
we smelled the acrid burning   of
rubber before we heard the squeal

of tires and the sickening crunch
of metal on metal,   our bodies
catapulted   as the car of another
evacuee   collided with ours.

Stuck in Blue Spring State Park, Florida

In Memory of Luther Lee Maloney

We slowly tread toward St. Johns River, rebelling
against the alluring warmth of Blue Spring
burgeoning below, where strangers dive deep
into an underwater cave, penetrating earth's secret,

subterranean hollows. The water's churning desire
to return to its source battled our innate urge for
autonomy, liberty, security, and the sweet feel of
gravity's chains anchoring our feet to solid ground.

Stumbling on the sandy shallows of the riverbed,
our bare feet disturbed slumbering soil, swirling
murky amber beneath the cerulean surface. Troubled,
the tributary carried on undaunted, flowing forward

to meet, to marry, to kiss the mouth of its betrothed,
that winding green river, and join the wedding march
to Mother Ocean, accompanied by an aggregation
of merry manatees, the buoyant, buxom bridal party.

Our labored breath gasped at sudden attack, our steps
stopped short, held hostage by a submerged log,
a trap thwarting any passage beyond its decay.
Our legs locked at the ankle like shackles, like home.

Nervous giggles filled the pause before panic
took root, bursting into anguished cries for help
from the family reunion we left in our quest for
adventure unknown in our small town, a world away.

Standing on the boardwalk with my cousin, Grandpa
saw us first, his smile widening at his wayward kin,
his bloodline, our lifeline, spanning the distance.
We waved and howled like wolves on the hunt.

While we, his imprisoned progeny, waited for rescue,
Grandpa waved back in blissful ignorance. Pointing
to the camera dangling from my cousin's neck,
he laughed: *The kids want you to take their picture!*

Whitetails in Wildflowers

Freckled twin fawns run
to graze in a sunlit field
wilded with flowers,

purpled with violets, irises,
ironweed, and Sweet
Williams, glowing yellow

with daffodils, dandelions,
and buttercups. Black-eyed
Susans bend to whisper

into the bejeweled ears
of Queen Anne's Lace,
tangling with goldenrod,

as bashful cherry blossoms
blush pink and surrender
their petals to the wind.

Catharsis

Death's daffodils are in full bloom,
hardy green and resplendent yellow,

pushed up through frozen soil, defying
cruel Winter's last fistful of snow.

Bulbs I planted in grief-stricken Autumn
have grown into Spring's sigh of relief—

a seedling keepsake of all we've lost
in unyielding seasons past, evolved.

Non-conformist Northern Flicker

While his kin live and work
in their natural habitat,
he refuses to conform.

I watch him defy instinct
to do as he pleases, this
solitary, obstinate bird—

a woodpecker by nature—
chiseling a stone wall
with his tiny, defiant beak.

Broken Wing Act

Killdeer bird eggs sleep, buried deep
in harsh gravel incubators, beneath
the married shadows of their parents,

silent sentries, standing elegant guard.
The softest sound of approaching threat
finds Father feigning winged injury,

his crooked trickster limp leading,
luring, predators away from his family.
This charade of nature, instinctual,

is called The Broken Wing Act.
No greater display of love exists
than self-sacrifice for your child.

IV

The Snow Angel

In the bleak midwinter[3]
on the year's coldest day,
an unwanted child was born.

Father prayed for a happy
accident, a miscarriage,
an abortion, an escape.

Mother simply prayed
for endurance, resigned
to melancholic motherhood.

The ties that bind bitterly
are a noose, choking
the infant marionette.

Farewell, sweet babe, farewell
'Til some distant 'morrow,
I am your future sorrow.

American Gothic

*She was not a Respectable Married Woman
but fully a human being*

-Sinclair Lewis, *Main Street.*

In the mountains of Appalachia,   at the dead end
of a muddy holler, stands a derelict farmhouse, where
weathered hands and calloused hearts   mold
                      a hardened, rotted monstrosity
              from the delicate clay   of matrimony.

He toils for naught in blue collar sweat.
He lives in a perpetual state of shrug,   tasting
neither the sweetness of joy   nor the bitter bite
                      of sorrow.
He chews her self-worth with razor sharp teeth,
cruel words further bruise   her already battered skin.
                          Insult added to injury.

Scraps of Scripture   falling, floating in mid-air;
her hidden Bible   unearthed, unbound,   a holy cloud
of confetti   torn by hand   for his ticker tape parade;
settling softly, silently beneath
                        their violent embrace.

He, the Hunter, mounts his trophy to the wall,
his steel trap fists locked   around her helpless wrists.
Caught, she, his captive   prey,   his trembling doe.
The eyewitness,   their hybrid fawn,   rent asunder by
                      their woodcut *danse macabre.*

    Fearing his mercurial wrath, his hair-trigger
shotgun, doe and fawn slipped the trap,   backwoods
refugees fleeing flesh and blood.   They rest in a
hidden hollow, a shelter of sympathy.

    The fawn cradled   in strange arms   as its
mother awaits judgement   on unforgiving,
dirty Welfare chairs carved of yellow plastic,
                                            a modern snare.

    The doe transformed   to domestic,   hired help
for pampered patrons of the poor.
    Her new perfume: the smell of bleach.

                    A scent so clean   he could not track.
                    A trail   so cold   he dare not follow.

Lessons in Mining

*Redneck referred to the red bandanas that
West Virginia miners wore around their necks.*

-Chuck Keeney, WV Mine Wars Museum.

In my Appalachian middle school, the teachers
transformed the classrooms   into a coal mining town.
A sylvan edition   of Stanford's Prison Experiment.

The rich students worked   for The Company,
while us poor kids played   the miner league.

Whether that division of labor   by social class
was preferential treatment   for the privileged   or
a broader lesson for all,   it lent an extra sting
to our respective roles   in the interactive project.

We miners had to crawl   on our hands and knees,
our necks   wrapped   in red bandanas—
                    identifying pennants
of our mining class   and filters for our breath—
into a dark "mine"   of cardboard boxes and blankets,
a ramshackle tunnel   smeared with black coal dust.

The teachers led us out quickly,   before our lungs
and minds were overtaken   by the polluted air
of the makeshift mineshaft.   Then they took us to

The Company Store,   doled out pieces of paper
Scrip,   and sent us forward   to barter for food   with
smug rich kids   wielding power   behind the counter.

The child of a poor, single mother, I was accustomed
to the bitterness   provoked
    by this lesson   in mining.

Choking in the cardboard coal mine   reminded me
of inhaling bleach fumes,   my face pressed against
my mother's clothes   as she hugged me,
my neck   wrapped   in her red hands—
                        her skin raw
from cleaning houses   of the town's elite, wealthy
parents whose children   looked down on me,
from their elevated posts   behind the counter.

The Company Store setup   felt much like waiting
with my mother   at the Welfare office.   The Scrip
like the stamps she was given   to trade for food.

It made me think   miners must be   like my mother,
parents   trading hard labor   in hazardous conditions,
doing whatever the world requires   of them
to keep their children   *warm and well fed.*[4]

The Ghosts We Inherit

The invisible felt   in tick tock pocket watch time,
hand wound in memory   of more innocent years.
When the word "family"   meant whole, meant safe—
or did it? Nostalgia is an unreliable narrator.

Rewind the tape,   let's play it again
to see what never happened.   The lies
we tell ourselves to sleep at night.   To look
ourselves in the mirror,   in the eyes

betraying truth   we're so desperate to hide.
Smell once more the hearth fire smoke,   taste
the fresh baked homemade fears   made quaint.
Photos reveal reality   as we choose to portray it.

You rebel, you miscreant, how dare you   breathe
a word unapproved by committee.   The open wound,
your mouth, a bloodletting   of secrets, a sin
that heaves hell   upon your own shoulders.

Uprooting what was planted   before your birth.
Setting a wildfire back through history,   a kindling
of your family tree, branches   turned to ash
by the match you lit, gnarled roots   no one wants

to see, buried so deep   not even hell can touch,
what lies beneath will devour us.   Better to
self-inflict revelation   than perpetuate heritage. Who
we are is what we do,   not the blood in our veins.

Ship of Theseus

they took away the old planks as they decayed,
putting in new and stronger timber in their place

-Plutarch

There was no funeral for my father.
No obituary, no fanfare. He died
on a Wednesday and gave his body

to Science. His widow proclaimed:
He always gave to other people.
His children, the proving exception.

His eyes now look out from inside
a stranger's skull.   Not that we could tell
one stranger   from another.

Who is my father now?   The gutted shell—
his original ship—or the unknown vessel
rebuilt   with his spare parts?

#NoFilter

  I've had enough of modern memory,
its obstinate insistence to spotlight bliss,
blurring imperfection into false beauty.
From Kodak moments to Instagram, *I am*
  half sick of shadows,[5] and light,
poses, posers, so much pretense.
For what? For whom? Who cares, when
    he is dead
and no one wants me to grieve.
I crave authenticity and ugliness,
recognition of the unsightly. Pretending
to be happy isn't happy, isn't anything,
so let's sulk together and exist. I feel
my years without shame, without applause,
happiness as acceptance, a raw nerve,
a shriek of crows in my throat, behold
my unabashed monstrosity, my blight
of truth. I'll take my pain over its absence.
Scars are proof of wounds, seedlings sown
for thicker skin. Such sweet music
veneers cacophony, a symphony, a howling.
My father once bought a bookshop's stock,
only to leave all of the books to rot, unread,
on the front porch until they were stolen.
I always hoped the thieves were readers.
Softly, the mist of memory overtakes me,
coloring false hues of joy over pain.
Boiled down to bones, the past may be
more palatable, but never properly digests.
Bleached stains are never as pure as origin.
I'd give anything to hear his voice again,
even shouting in anger. I barely knew him,
but I miss the what-if of him, the what
could've been of him, of us.

I traveled the world. I made new memories
I can't bear   to speak of. I've lived too hard
for polite dinner conversation. I abhor
small talk and small minds. They need me
to be familiar. I need them   to disappear.
    Celebrate   the aftermath, the hangover,
the what really happened.
        I still don't want to see it.

V

Neighborhood Watch

There goes the Devil,
splitting fences   like an axe-
wielding lunatic.   While over there
   stands the witness
to his crimes,   her eyes
have seen it all,   though her memory
has grown as gray   as her wiry hair.
A dumb dog runs   straight into the path
of an oncoming truck,   which veers
to the right, right   into her mailbox,
then a fire hydrant.   Unread letters
and utility bills fly,   bursting
into the air like confetti,   like the kids
running, jumping with joy,   arms out-
stretched   to catch whatever fun they can.
Let it be!   She shouts at them
from her front porch rocking chair.
   The devil sees your greed!
We don't know our own faces
in the dark   beyond the streetlights.
The houses blush bright pink to think of it.
But she'll speak truth   and shame
   the Devil.

Shadowbox

The fleeting given,   you are grateful
for the brevity   as much as the bestowal,
the sage advice,   the marrow, the clawed out
eyes   of your anxiety—   if our outsides
matched our insides,   everyone would scream
and run away—   a tiny wish stays hidden,
penitent remains,   let us be as divided
as a wishbone,   picked clean by scavengers.
I've lost the plot.
                              You empathize
the homeless woman   hiding her trove
under a butterfly bush   in the parking lot
of your corporate office,   still
you turn away,   so your privilege won't hurt
her pride,   or vice versa.
Our eyes take in   what our brains can't process
for our mouths to say.   Why don't we do
anything   of substance?
We have always hated   mirrors
for reflecting   our flaws.

Bonfires

Good fences make good neighbors

-Robert Frost

Give us today   our daily medication,
and may we forgive   those who trespass
our property   before we find our shotguns.

The news is all bad   all the time,
so why bother   learning anything
we don't already know.

In mid-summer,   we witness a murder
of crows   cloak a dead tree in darkness
How green the grass grows

on the neighbor's lawn,   as he
pukes   last night's beer
over the white picket fence.

Gaggles of stars   shoot across
our bows,   our furrowed brows,
a warning   of woes to come.

From sea to shining   swamp,
the air we breathe   is a tinderbox
and our raised torches   are lit.

The Evening News

Gunshot stain
on a tranquil town.

Fear locks doors once left open
for neighbors and strangers alike

to warm by hearth fires
and share a kind meal.

Small town gossip frozen stiff
and cold as the fresh corpse

on a manicured lawn, a blood-
soaked flower garden.

No one sleeps now.
No one smiles now.

No children playing.
No faithful praying.

Time stands still on a Main Street corner
of a community in shell shock, caught

unprepared for the grim reality
of human nature.

Ism

*A cat's cradle is nothing but a bunch of X's
between somebody's hands...
No damn cat, and no damn cradle.*

        -Kurt Vonnegut, Jr. *Cat's Cradle.*

A giant, twisting rollercoaster
snakes across the nation.
People stand in a winding queue
stretched beyond the horizon.

How eagerly they wait,
to be taken   for a ride
for everyone else is going &
nobody wants to be left behind.

So they line up, a crowd
of lonely people taking selfies,
zombie cattle, sheep
ready and willing to be led
to the slaughter.

For the thrill ride ends
in a gauntlet of guillotines
—machetes swinging down
from twisted vines above—

slicing up the smorgasbord
of the gullible,
        so delectable,
into cold, raw cuts
of bloody naivety.

Democratic Pomp

Remember the bliss of ignorance?
Indifference and the innocence of youth,
rosy cheeks of self-centered freedom?
Before you were told: *You can change the world.*

So you protest the war on humanity,
the so-called king and his menagerie.
But all I see are rich men
and their game of tug-o-war,
struggling for power and photo ops.

Now you stand on opposite sides
screaming, raging, waving flags
of hatred and holding up signs
with no conviction. For what choice
is the lesser of two evils?

Oh yes, that *banner yet waves*[6]
over the eyes of the free
and the mouths of the brave.

The Ethics of Horses

The general ethos of the people they have to govern determines the behavior of politicians.

-T.S. Eliot

Ethos arose from
the habitats of horses.[7]
As if moral character was
steadfast, a fixed point
of reference, of shelter, of home,
yet something lowly, a beast
of burden beneath man.
No wonder, then, he has
produced such pedigreed
jackasses to coronate as kings,
while we sit, stillife in stables,
rotting from their rhetoric.

Avaricious Symbiosis

Axiom breath of dead lungs, the calm
bombastic births a delicate cacophony.
Imagine the illusion of incandescence,
mesmeric, effulgence over a chasm.
Juxtapose an artless, xenophobic
greeting, devoid of empathy, with a fire
-fighter holding a child in an old photograph.
How far beneath us is gratitude, dignity
of language, of verbal silk?
Can a knife be neutral in any hand?
Farewell my kaleidoscopic forgiveness,
reality supersedes trust underneath the bruise.
Yonder is the last civilization
in a zoo no one cares to visit.

Give the Bard a Hep A Shot

None of our employees has Hepatitis!
brags the handwritten sign hanging
on the door of the local Piggly Wiggly.

Skull face drug mules walk on, hauling
big backpacks on shoulders so sharp
and boney it's a wonder they don't break,

to the fast food joint on the corner,
which doesn't bear a Hep A status sign,
making their drop at the drive-thru window.

The news says it's ok, it's rare to catch Hep A
from food service workers. Still, they keep
an updated list of each diagnosis. Today,

another overdose at the school playground,
where a student stepped on a used needle.
The news says it's ok, it didn't break the skin.

VI

In Search of a Karass

> *humanity is organized into teams...a karass ignores national, institutional, occupational, familial, and class boundaries*
>
> -Kurt Vonnegut, Jr. *Cat's Cradle.*

The carcass
        lays
               sprawled
    across a mist-
     cloaked field.

Mildewed tents, rusty
      cages,   the bones
   of an abandoned
carnival,   'twined in dead
      grass and discarded serpent skin.

   When unchecked weeds, wild and
carnivorous, swallowed
       sad
children whole, neighbors turned
          their faces away.

One man's indifference is another's shame. Blame
passes   through every set of lips
   until the next bite.

Drops of blood
      on a snowdrift,
      on my palms, on the wheel, driving
         cross-country to reach
ocean, my spleen a piece of sea
        glass.   Still,
   it shall be vented.

Driftwood

It's true you can't ever go home again.

Once you've been to Earth's razor edge,
the scenic overlook to human hell,
     home becomes a foreign country
you wake up in, jetlagged and groggy,
without a passport, and you just
          drank the ~~Kool-Aid~~ water.

Even when you stand in your mother's kitchen,
surrounded by laughing family and friends,
or sit at your nondescript desk in a fluorescent-lit office
    doing routine work in your ordinary life,
you will never be normal again.   Never home.
You will forever be marked as Other. Elsewhere.

A secret, scarred, splintered piece of driftwood.

    Adrift, always, on a post-traumatic sea.

Solastalgia

*Solastalgia: the distress caused
by environmental change.*

- Glenn Albrecht, PhD

The small town seemed smaller
when I finally returned—the mountains,
the airport,   the two-lane highway,
   even my mother's shoulders
as she gave me a welcome home hug.

Every place in my memory   was gone.
My grade school,   my high school,
the town's lone, vintage gas pump,
and the tiny, square hotdog stand,   once
the social hub   of our community.

What hadn't been destroyed   by fire, flood,
storms, and chemical spills,   had withered
away   and disappeared   as disasters
and death   drove droves away—
a mass exodus   of Appalachians.

I sailed around the world   only to find
that I am now the one   left behind,
without an anchor,   haunted
   and homesick   for a home
that no longer exists.

Crossroads

I sat upon the Royal Canal bridge, staring
up at stars flung over silent fields, praying
desperately to God for solace and daring
the Devil when no answer came, standing
up to take the leap into oblivion, stopping
when I heard His voice call my name.

Glendalough

Grey, rain-soaked clouds hang, thick
and thunderous, dark veils in weary skies
far above the lush green Wicklow Mountains.

The crowded bus rocks on dirty wheels, speeding
along the tiny dirt road that snakes and curls
around ancient trees and empty stone churches.

The two lakes of Glendalough appear, cradling
the abandoned monastery, its pristine water
circled by craggy rocks and broken trails.

Its venerable history lost to the multitude
of pilgrims flocking, praying among ruins and
crumbling headstones below the round tower.

Grasping at fragile faith, the modern world
intrudes, profaning sacred graves of forgotten
Saints and Sinners and The Unknown.

Seafarers

Some say Saint Brendan traveled
from Ireland to West Virginia
long before Columbus ever set sail.
Perhaps that's why the Criel and
Grave Creek burial mounds of the
Adena bear a ghostly resemblance
to the Neolithic earthen domes of
Brú na Bóinne. The solstice sun
kisses Ogham petroglyphs in the
Tug River Valley on its overseas
journey to the triskel-carved cover
stone of Newgrange, soft beams of
light illuminating the passage tomb
through the corbel arch, bouncing
between bookended emeralds, the
green-hued mountains and waters
of Glen Ferris and Glendalough.

The Parting Glass

So fill to me the parting glass
Good night and joy be with you all

(traditional)

In Harper's Ferry, where the town
square's antiquated shops still
smoke after desecration by fire,
two rivers converge, crowned by
Blue Ridge Mountains, crossed by
steel and timber railroad bridges.
The Appalachian Trail imbibes
the Potomac panorama before
its trek into northern wilderness
and transatlantic ocean immersion
end at the Irish coast, sliding up
the Slieve League cliffs of Donegal
and down the Sperrin Mountains of
Tyrone to grab a Guinness in an
Ulster pub, toasting every glorious
mountain climbed between the
rivers Shenandoah and Shannon.

Playlist

Give the Bard a Tetanus Shot Spotify Playlist:

http://spoti.fi/2OUFS0K

Acknowledgements

Thanks to my editor, Freddy La Force, for believing in my work. Thanks also to the following publications, in which variations of these poems first appeared:

Poet Lore:	"No Trespassing"
Barzakh:	"Give the Bard a Tetanus Shot"
Southword:	"Formative"
Five:2:One:	"Fire-tongued Labyrinth"
Spillway:	"Snow Cream"
Tar River Poetry:	"Trestle"
Undeniable: Writers Respond to Climate Change Anthology (Alternating Current Press):	"Watershed"
Big Muddy:	"The Stone Age"
Entropy:	"Tilt-A-Whirl" & "Broken Wing Act"
Looking at Appalachia:	"For Want of an Ark"
Barren Magazine:	"Flood Diorama"
Still:	"Baptism by Fire"
Appalachian Journal:	"Cover Us with Mountains"
From the Depths (Haunted Waters Press):	"The Farm"
Yellow Chair Review:	"His Orchestra"
Firewords Quarterly:	"Hibernation"
Emerging Writers of the Southeast Anthology (Z Publishing):	"Hinterland"
Euphony:	"Non-conformist Northern Flicker"
Rust + Moth:	"The Snow Angel"
Queen Mob's Teahouse:	"American Gothic"
New Southern Fugitives:	"Lessons in Mining" & "Bonfires"
The Minnesota Review:	"Ship of Theseus"
The Hellebore:	"Shadowbox"
Labyrinth:	"The Evening News"
So It Goes (Kurt Vonnegut Memorial Museum & Library):	"Ism"
The Pedestal:	"Democratic Pomp"
The Cape Rock:	"The Ethics of Horses"
The Galway Review:	"Avaricious Symbiosis" & "Crossroads"
Barnhouse:	"Give the Bard a Hep A Shot"
The Maine Review:	"In Search of a Karass"
Routine Anthology (Crack the Spine Press):	"Driftwood"
Potomac Review:	"Solastalgia"
Falling Star:	"Glendalough"
Appalachian Heritage:	"Seafarers" & "The Parting Glass"

Poet's Bio

V.C. Myers is an Appalachian poet whose work has appeared in many literary journals around the world, including *Poet Lore, Prairie Schooner, The Minnesota Review, Appalachian Heritage,* and *Tar River Poetry. Give the Bard a Tetanus Shot* is her debut collection.

Notes

[1] Wilder, Thornton. *Our Town*. 1938.
[2] Shakespeare, William. *Hamlet*. 4.5.4243.
[3] Rossetti, Christina. *In the Bleak Midwinter*. 1872.
[4] James 2:16. *NWT*. 1984.
[5] Tennyson, Alfred. *The Lady of Shalott*. 1832.
[6] Key, Francis Scott. *The Star-spangled Banner*. 1814.
[7] Homer. *Iliad.* 6.511.

www.ingramcontent.com/pod-product-compliance
Lightning Source LLC
Chambersburg PA
CBHW070156080526
44586CB00015B/2015